All About Your ...

Contents

Sensational Shepherds! — 2
The positives; The negatives; The adult dog; Coat and colours; What's in a name?; The breed's pioneer.

Choosing A German Shepherd — 6
Finding a breeder; Assessing the puppies: Male or female.

Picking Your Puppy — 10
Show potential; The companion GSD; Working dogs.

Getting Ready — 12
A place to sleep; Indoor crate; Outdoor run.

Collecting Your Puppy — 14
Arriving home; House training.

The Right Start — 16
Socialisation; Feeding; Exercise; Car travel.

Training Your German Shepherd — 20
Lead training; Sit; Come; Down; Stay; Further training.

Caring For Your German Shepherd — 26
Grooming; Nails; Teeth.

Health Care — 28
Vaccinations; Worming; Fleas; Bloat; Anal furunculosis; Joint problems.

Sensational Shepherds!

Intelligent, loyal, dependable, sensible, quick to learn... these are some of the characteristics that have made the German Shepherd Dog one of the most popular breeds in the world.

If you want to know more about his background and character, and how to choose, care for and train a German Shepherd, then this is the book for you.

First things first – are you sure a German Shepherd will fit in with your lifestyle? Thousand of devotees will tell you that the GSD's unique personality makes him a pet without parallel, but nevertheless you should consider both advantages and disadvantages very carefully before making your decision.

THE POSITIVES
Temperament
The German Shepherd is used worldwide as a police dog because his loyal temperament and guarding ability can be ideally harnessed for protection work. This blend of characteristics makes the German Shepherd a fine companion dog who will look after both home and family.

Most Shepherds get on well with children, particularly if they are brought up with them.

The German Shepherd is also used extensively as a Guide Dog for the Blind, and the breed's intelligence and initiative have proved a great asset in this line of work.

The German Shepherd is used by police forces throughout the world.

Trainability
Highly intelligent and eager to please, the German Shepherd can be trained to reach levels of performance beyond the reach of most breeds. However, it is important to bear in mind that the German Shepherd has a sensitive nature, and sympathetic, tactful handling is essential in order to get the best from your dog.

THE NEGATIVES
Maintenance
The GSD is a large, powerful dog that requires plenty of regular exercise. If you don't like walking, try another breed.

Mental exercise is as important as physical exercise, and the keen intelligence of the German Shepherd must be utilised or you will end up with a bored, unhappy dog (see page 20).

The German Shepherd has a double, weather-resistant coat... and your carpets and furniture may soon be able to boast the same! Most GSDs shed their coat twice a year, and that means *a lot* of dog hair. A daily groom will certainly help.

The highly intelligent German Shepherd needs plenty of mental stimulation.

Temperament
The German Shepherd has a tendency to form a particular bond with one member of the family, usually the person who feeds and trains him. However, most GSDs will interact well with everyone in the household. That strong guarding instinct means your Shepherd will almost always bark when strangers approach the house.

Sensational Shepherds!

The typical dark, rich colours of the German Shepherd.

The Adult Dog

The average mature male grows to about 25 inches (approximately 64 cm) at the withers (top of the shoulder), and weighs around 80 pounds (36 kg). Bitches are usually some two inches smaller and correspondingly lighter. Life expectancy is around 12 years.

Coat And Colour

German Shepherds come in a variety of beautiful colours, the most usual being a black saddle with tan or gold markings. All black, all grey, or grey with lighter or brown markings (which are known as sables) are also quite common and are acceptable in the show ring. White German Shepherds cannot be shown under present dog show rules, but this could change if the proponents of this variety are successful.

Correctly, the German Shepherd should have a short, flat outer coat with a thick undercoat, providing maximum protection against the weather. Long-coated Shepherds are popular with pet owners, but they are unlikely to be successful in the show ring. Coat type becomes apparent at around six weeks, so the choice is a matter of personal preference.

Sables are grey with lighter or brown markings.

What's In A Name?

The German Shepherd Dog (*Deutsche Schäferhunde*), naturally enough, originated in Germany. As its name also suggests, the breed was used to work with sheep. Predators were a great threat to the European sheep industry 200 years ago, and a dog was needed that could both herd and defend the flock.

The development of a 'shepherd dog' was done without sophisticated scientific studies; the shepherd would simply mate his best working bitch to the best working dog on the neighbouring farm. Consequently the breed evolved in a huge variety of shapes, sizes and colours.

The Breed's Pioneer

The modern German Shepherd was born in 1899, when a cavalry captain, Max von Stephanitz, formed the first internationally recognised GSD breed club, the *Verein für Deutsche Schäferhunde*. A Standard for the breed – a written blueprint for correct appearance and temperament – was drawn up in Germany and has remained virtually unchanged in the 100 years since.

The breed was widely used by the German army in the Great War (1914 to 1918), and later, returning British and American soldiers brought dogs home with them. In no time, the popularity of the German Shepherd soared in both countries, and it soon became a favourite worldwide. Interestingly, the breed was known as the Alsatian in Britain for many years, to avoid prejudice against its German origins.

The long-coated German Shepherd.

Choosing A German Shepherd

Now you have decided to take the plunge and go out and buy a German Shepherd puppy, you want to make absolutely certain that you make the right choice.

The best plan is to gather as much information as you can. Contact your national Kennel Club and try to locate a dog show in your area where German Shepherds will be exhibited. Then go along and take a look at the adults on show to get an idea of the type of dog you are looking for. Approach the owners of the dogs. They may not have puppies available, but most German Shepherd fanciers are more than happy to talk about the breed that is their passion! They will answer your questions and give advice if required.

It is important to find out as much as possible about the breed – from puppyhood through to old age – so you would be well-advised to tap into all sources of information. This can include books, videos and the internet.

Take time to do your homework before rushing out to buy a puppy.

You should be given the opportunity to see the puppies with their mother.

Finding A Breeder

Whether you want a German Shepherd as a companion, a working dog or a show dog, it is important to locate a breeder with a reputation for producing sound, healthy, good-quality puppies. Your national Kennel Club will put you in touch with the GSD breed club in your area, and the breed club secretary will often know which breeders have puppies for sale.

When you have found a breeder, do not be afraid to ask questions about both the puppies, and their parents. Ask the breeder how long he/she has been involved with GSDs, and find out as much as you can about their breeding lines. A genuine breeder will be happy to answer your questions.

DID YOU KNOW?

A grey German Shepherd puppy dog, born in the trenches under fire during World War I, was taken back to the United States and later became a famous dog superstar, Rin Tin Tin.

Choosing A German Shepherd

Watch the puppies play together to get an idea of individual personalities.

DID YOU KNOW?

In Germany as early as 1911, there were over 400 police stations provided with specially trained German Shepherd Dogs.

Assessing The Puppies

It is most important to check that the parents of the puppies have been tested for hip dysplasia (see page 31). Ideally, you should see both parents, but this is not always possible as the sire may live at the other end of the country. However, you should certainly be able to see the mother with her puppies. Watching how the puppies interact with each other and with their mother will give you a good indication of temperament. It is also interesting to see other related members of the family to get an idea of what the adult temperament is like.

Do not be surprised if the breeder also asks you lots of questions: Where do you live? Are you at work all day? What are your plans for the puppy? Responsible breeders are genuinely concerned about the people buying their puppies and what kind of life they will offer.

Male Or Female?

If you want a family companion and you are planning to keep your dog in the house, a bitch has the advantage of being smaller and less powerfully built than a male. However, a well-trained German Shepherd knows his place, and will not get under your feet like some of the smaller, less obedient breeds.

We find there is little difference between the sexes when it comes to faithfulness; both make very loyal family members. Bitches have the disadvantage of going into season, usually every six months, and unless you plan to spay her, you will need to keep your bitch away from male dogs during this time. Anti-mate sprays cannot be depended on. Spaying is more effective as a means of preventing unwanted pregnancy, and other health complications. Ask your vet for advice as to when is the most suitable time to carry out this operation.

If you plan to show your German Shepherd, a bitch is probably the best choice as, if you have a good specimen with no outstanding faults of temperament or conformation, and free from hereditary disorders, you also have the option of breeding from her.

A male (left) is bigger and more powerfully built than a bitch.

Picking Your Puppy

Show Potential

If you want a show puppy, you must tell the breeder as early as possible so that he/she can help you to select one of suitable quality. That means the puppy is of good conformation, with a sound temperament. It should have the correct coat, with dark, rich colours, and be sturdy and healthy in appearance.

When we are selling puppies that have show potential we never guarantee anything, except that the puppy is displaying the promise to make the show ring. For every puppy that has this potential for showing probably no more than five per cent will actually win in the ring.

Remember that if you want your adult Shepherd to have a nice saddle, then you must choose a puppy at around eight weeks with plenty of black colouring on the face, (especially the muzzle) and all over the body to the top of the legs.

When first born, this puppy would, to the inexperienced eye, appear almost completely black, but on closer inspection, the eyebrows would be gold and possibly the feet. Therefore by the time your puppy is a year old he should be a good black and gold colouring.

A puppy may be sold with show potential – but there is no guarantee of success. This is Ch. Jonimay Shannan, a major influence at stud and in the show ring.

The Companion GSD

It may seem difficult to distinguish the companion puppy from the show puppy, especially if you have selected a good breeder who only breeds from quality bitches. The breeder will have used a top-class dog to complement the bitch, so do not think that because you are buying a non-show puppy that he will not make an excellent specimen on reaching maturity. The fine points of perfection make winners in the show ring, but these technical features are not of great importance to the owner who wants a good-looking, pet-quality Shepherd.

A sound temperament is paramount, and the pet owner should always go for the happy, extrovert puppy that shows no hint of nervousness.

Working Dogs

All dogs, whether show, working or companion, benefit from training in elementary obedience, but if you plan to compete in Obedience, Agility or Working Tests, you will be looking for that little bit extra. Go for the puppy that is full of mischief, showing curiosity in everything that is going on. Try playing with a toy, and see which puppy runs out to retrieve it. Better still, see if the puppy will pick up your car keys and run around with them.

Getting Ready

Make sure the toys you buy are both safe and durable.

Most breeders allow their puppies to go to their new homes at around eight weeks of age, but there is plenty you can do to get ready for the new arrival. Firstly, make sure your home is safe for him. This means checking that electrical wires are out of reach and ensuring the garden is secure. If you have a swimming pool or fish pond, it should be fenced off.

It is important you have the basic equipment. This is what we recommend:
- Two stainless steel bowls
- Comb
- Grooming glove
- Toys (safe and durable)
- Leather lead and an adjustable puppy collar.

When your puppy has outgrown his puppy collar, we suggest using a long-linked choke chain (approximately 22 to 24 inches long for a female and 24 to 26 inches for a male). Do not buy a fine-linked or round-linked choke, as over a period or time this will wear away the hair on one side of the neck, leaving a gap in the coat.

A Place To Sleep

Your puppy will also want something to sleep in. There are plenty of beds of all sizes and prices on the market. To begin with, a cardboard box lined with an old blanket is perfectly adequate, but a large, strong, plastic bed is probably the best buy. It is easy to clean and disinfect. Buy two pieces of bedding so that one is always clean.

A plastic bed is easy to keep clean.

If your puppy is sleeping in the house, be sure you select a quiet corner in a room where he has some privacy. Put his bed in a draught-proof area, and choose a location where you don't have to keep disturbing him once he has settled down to sleep.

Indoor Crate

A collapsible wire crate is a good investment... it just might save you a small fortune in chewed carpets and furniture. The crate can be used at night and is also useful for containing your puppy for short periods during the day.

If you have children, a crate provides the puppy with a sanctuary when he wants to get away for a bit of peace and quiet. It also helps with house training and provides a safe means of transporting your dog in the car.

Outside Run

We advise pet owners, when possible, to build a run in the garden. This is the puppy's own space, and can be used for all the same reasons as the indoor crate.

Collecting Your Puppy

When the day finally arrives to collect your puppy you need the following documents from the breeder: a pedigree, a Kennel Club registration certificate, and a diet sheet. You should also be provided with details of worming treatments to date.

You will need to know what the breeder has been feeding him on so that you can have the same diet awaiting his arrival. Most breeders will be happy to give you food for the first one or two meals.

Despite all the excitement of bringing your new friend home, you must remember that this is a very traumatic time for the puppy. It is a bewildering experience for the youngster to be parted from his littermates and taken to a strange environment. It is therefore important to ensure that this is not accompanied by introducing strange food to his diet, as a stomach upset will inevitably result.

Arriving Home

Take time to introduce your new puppy to his surroundings and be sure to take him outside to relieve himself. He will now meet all the members of his family, which may include children and other pets. Make sure all introductions are carefully supervised, and try not to overwhelm your puppy with too much attention. Play with him, by all means, but do not overdo it. When he tires, ensure that he is left alone to sleep.

The first night can be a trying experience for new puppy and new owner. Without the company of his brothers and sisters, your German Shepherd will feel abandoned and is almost sure to cry.

Try leaving a radio playing to help the settling-in process, but don't be surprised if a trip to the kitchen in the middle of the night is necessary to offer comfort. Don't despair... it does get easier.

House Training

This is a top priority, and you should start training your German Shepherd from day one. An eight-week-old puppy will need to relieve himself very regularly throughout the day, so he should be taken out to a chosen spot in the garden every couple of hours. In addition, he should be taken out as soon as he wakes up, after every meal, after playing, and before he goes to bed. If you see him squatting at any time, take him outside straight away. When he is on his spot, use a command such as "Busy" or "Be clean," and your intelligent German Shepherd pup will soon learn to associate the word with the deed.

If your puppy has an accident, never punish him, as he will not understand what he has done wrong, and will get very upset. You will just have to be more vigilant in the future, and take him out more often.

Remember, if he gets it wrong, it is probably your fault.

Supervise introductions, especially with small children.

15

The Right Start

DID YOU KNOW?

In Germany, a German Shepherd Dog cannot be shown in the breed ring after its second birthday, unless it has working qualifications.

Socialisation

All puppies need to be socialised to get used to all the things they may encounter in the course of everyday life, and this is especially crucial for German Shepherds, who may be wary of anything they have never encountered before.

Let your German Shepherd pup explore everything and encourage him to do so. When he first arrives home, let him inspect your home at his own pace. If he approaches an unusual object, such as a vacuum cleaner, mop and bucket, etc., encourage him to investigate and show him there is nothing to

Make sure your puppy is exposed to as many different situations as possible.

The well-socialised German Shepherd will learn to be tolerant and obedient.

be afraid of. Once he has sniffed the unfamiliar object, give him a treat and a cuddle so he associates it with a positive experience.

Your German Shepherd should meet as many people as possible, so invite visitors around to play and interact with the puppy – you don't usually have to ask twice!

After his second inoculation has taken effect (see page 28), he will be ready to investigate the outside world and all its sounds and smells. Introduce him to as many new things as you can – motorcycles, pushchairs, anything that could frighten him when he is older.

DID YOU KNOW?

The original breed club in Germany, the Verein für Deutsche Schäferhunde (SV) was founded in 1899. At that time it had 31 members; after 10 years it had approximately 10,000; after 20 years it had between 40,000 to 50,000 members. Today the membership is above 100,000, making it the largest single breed club in the world.

The Right Start

Feeding

German Shepherd pups need a good diet if they are to grow into big, strong, healthy dogs. Remember that fresh water should always be available. Most puppies are fed four meals a day. As the puppy grows, he will become less interested in some of his meals, and they can be cut down to two meals (morning and evening). Some owners cut down to one meal eventually.

If you wish to change what your pup is fed, this should be done very gradually to give your Shepherd's stomach time to adjust to the new food. This should not be done during the first few days when he is still settling down in his new home. Add just a tiny amount of the new food to his meal. Gradually, over the course of a couple of weeks, increase the amount added, and decrease the amount of his previous food, until eventually a complete change-over has taken place.

There are many different types of food that can be fed. Some owners prefer a 'meat and biscuits' diet, others favour 'complete' diets which offer a nutritionally balanced meal. Some complete foods are aimed at the different life stages of the dog – from puppyhood and into old age, ensuring your German Shepherd's changing needs are always catered for.

If your German Shepherd pup has diarrhoea, feed a light diet of chicken and rice. If it doesn't clear up within 24 hours, or if you are at all concerned about your pup's health, seek veterinary advice.

To begin with, your puppy will need four meals a day.

Exercise

For the first five to six months of life, exercise should be kept to a minimum. This is vitally important in a large breed like the German Shepherd. If you over-exercise at this stage, it could lead to serious problems. Bones do not fully calcify until the puppy is about nine months old, and so excessive or inappropriate exercise can damage bones and joints.

Apart from playing with your German Shepherd pup in the garden, go for short walks at a steady pace and alway keep your puppy on the lead. Once your dog is over six months old, you can build up his exercise, increasing the length of walks and introducing free-running, as long as you are in a safe place and you have trained your dog to come back to you.

Limit exercise to short outings on the lead while your puppy is going through the vulnerable growing period.

Car Travel

After a few short journeys, most German Shepherd puppies have little problems with travel, but some take longer to become accustomed to the car.

When taking your puppy out for the first time in the car, make it a short journey. Just drive down to your local shops, take him out when you get there, if only for a few minutes, then put him back in the car and go home again (make sure he's had his inoculations first).

Remember that dogs should never be left unattended in a car. Even on an overcast day, cars can quickly heat up, and many dogs have been known to die of heatstroke.

Training Your German Shepherd

Training is great fun, especially with a German Shepherd, who is so intelligent and eager to learn. The most important thing to bear in mind is that the GSD is a very sensitive breed and does not respond well to being punished or shouted at. By nature, the Shepherd will do his very best to please his owner, and any form of harsh treatment will damage this relationship

The best way of encouraging your pup to learn is to make training enjoyable by rewarding good behaviour (with praise and a small treat) and by ignoring inappropriate behaviour.

The intelligent German Shepherd is quick to learn and will enjoy the stimulation of training.

Do not try to do too much at once, and always finish the session while your puppy is still enjoying it and wanting to do more. The German Shepherd may focus on one member of the family, and this is likely to be the person who does most of the training and exercising. However, your Shepherd should learn that he must respect and obey all members of the 'family pack'. So try to ring the changes and allow other family members to do a few training exercises, making sure they have plenty of treats on hand to encourage a good response.

Lead Training

Before lead training, your German Shepherd pup should be used to wearing a light collar. The next step is take him out to the garden, where you have enough space to work. Sit him on your left-hand side, put a lead on him, and encourage him to walk forward by holding a treat or a toy in front of him. As he walks beside you, say "Heel" and praise him. If he pulls too far ahead, stop, put him in the right position, and start again. Eventually, he should learn the Heel command, and will walk beside you without the need of treats or toys. This exercise can be practised before your puppy has completed his vaccination course, so that he will be walking confidently on the lead when he is ready to go for walks outside the home.

Lead training can start in the garden while you are waiting for your pup to complete his vaccination course.

DID YOU KNOW?

Louis XI, who ruled in France early in the 15th century, was the first to use dogs for civic protection. He provided the famous town of Mont St. Michel and later St. Malo with a dog corps.

Training Your German Shepherd

The Sit is taught by holding a treat above the puppy's head, which encourages him to look up and then go into the Sit position.

Sit

Hold a treat and show it to your German Shepherd. He will follow your hand with his nose in an attempt to take the treat. Put your hand above his head, in such a position that, to reach the treat, he has to stretch his head up and back a little and his bottom must go down on the floor. As soon as this happens, say "Sit", give him the treat, and make a big fuss of him.

Come

To train your German Shepherd puppy to return to you, get one of the family to hold him in the Sit position a few yards away from you. Hold his food bowl (with one of his meals in it), show it to the pup, call his name, and give the command "Come" in an excited tone of voice to encourage him to you. When he arrives in front of you, give him the bowl and praise him.

Once your German Shepherd has the basic idea, the bowl can be replaced with a toy or a treat. When he is familiar with this exercise, ask him to Come, and then to Sit before he gets the treat.

Down

Hold a treat in your hand so that only a small amount of it is showing, and put your hand on the floor. The pup will try every way to get the treat, and will eventually realise that he needs to lie down in order to get closer to it. As soon as he does, say "Down", give him the treat, and make him feel very special and clever.

To begin with, a treat is used to guide the puppy into the Down position.

Training Your German Shepherd

Stay

Now you have got your puppy responding to the recall, you can practise the Stay exercise. Start with your puppy in the Sit, and then gradually build up the distance you leave your puppy. Use a hand signal to keep the pup in position.

Do not call the puppy to you at the end of the exercise, but return to his side and gently praise him while he stays in the Sit.

As your puppy gets more proficient, you can introduce distractions such as doing a Stay exercise with another dog.

The German Shepherd is at his happiest when he is working with his owner.

Further Training

Once you have experienced the pleasure of getting your German Shepherd to obey commands, you may want to start more intensive work with a local training club. This also gives you the opportunity to socialise with other dogs.

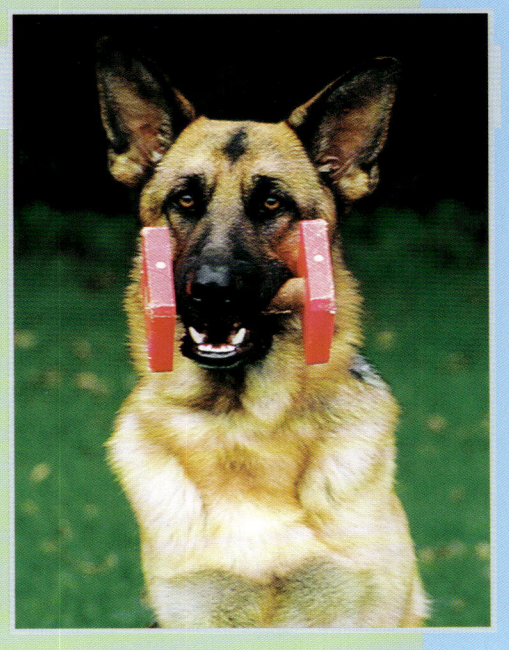

The German Shepherd is such an intelligent, highly-motivated dog, that mental stimulation is essential to his well-being. It is highly recommended that you train your Shepherd in one of the many disciplines available, such as Obedience, Agility, Working Trials, Flyball, or Show training. There is something to suit everyone – and your German Shepherd will respond to all new challenges that are put his way.

Your German Shepherd will enjoy the mental and physical stimulation of Agility work.

Caring For Your German Shepherd

Grooming

Just a few minutes' thorough grooming every day will keep your dog clean and leave a shine on his coat. A German Shepherd coat is a double coat. The thick undercoat is a woolly texture and the top coat is dense and straight.

Your adult German Shepherd will lose his coat about twice a year. The top coat will probably look rather dull and he may even lose a few pounds in weight, but do not worry because this is quite normal; as soon as he has finished shedding, he will put the weight back on and the coat will recover its usual lustre.

If your dog gets into a muddy mess after a long walk, let it dry then comb and brush it out. If he is just too muddy, fill a bucket with warm water and wash your dog down all over, rinse with clean warm water, and dry thoroughly with a towel. Once you have finished, put plenty of newspaper down and let your German Shepherd lie on them to soak up any excess moisture from his underparts. Once he is dry, a quick brush will leave him gleaming.

If you accustom your puppy to being groomed from an early age, he will never resent the attention.

Nails

Your German Shepherd's nails should be kept short. Examine them regularly, and cut them with guillotine-type nail clippers if they are too long. Be sure not to cut the dark quick of the nail, as this will bleed and will be very painful to your dog. If in doubt, ask a vet to show you how to clip the nails safely.

Teeth

Puppies lose their milk teeth when they are between 4-6 months of age. Some youngsters get through this stage with few problems, others suffer from sore gums, and there are those that take the art of chewing to an art form while they are teething. In all cases, make sure that you do not play rough tug-of-war type games with your pup during this time.

An adult's teeth should be cleaned regularly to prevent tooth decay, gum disease and bad breath. A toothbrush or a fingerbrush can be used, together with tasty toothpaste designed for dogs. Get your pup used to having his teeth cleaned, so it will not be too much of a struggle when he is older.

The occasional large bone, one that cannot be splintered, is also a good way of promoting healthy teeth.

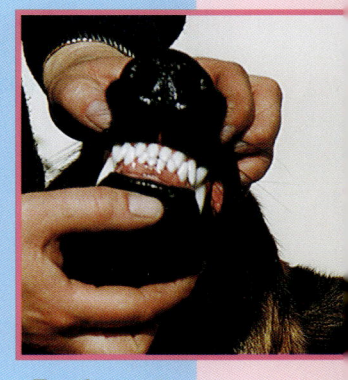

Teeth must be kept clean in order to avoid decay and gum disease.

Ear carriage may be affected during teething.

Health Care

Before buying your German Shepherd, you should have already investigated the conditions to which the breed can be prone (e.g. heart problems, joint problems and auto-immune problems) and should have checked that the parents' lines are as healthy as possible. Your vet will give you details of what to check for in the breed, and any health certificates that you should ask to see. Make sure your vet is knowledgeble about the breed and understands hip scoring requirements.

When you get your puppy, take him to the vet to be checked over. You should also use the opportunity to talk to the vet about any problems which you should look out for. Never take risks with your German Shepherd's health. If you are at all concerned about your dog, be on the safe side and seek immediate veterinary advice.

Vaccinations

There are a number of infectious diseases that affect dogs – all of which can be avoided with a comprehensive vaccination programme. Your German Shepherd needs protection against distemper, infectious hepatitis, parvovirus, leptospirosis, and rabies (excluding Britain). Your vet will advise you when the inoculations should be given, depending on locality and incidence of disease. Generally, the first injection is given at around eight weeks, with a second injection at 12 weeks. An annual booster will be needed thereafter.

Worming

Your breeder should have wormed the puppy several times before you purchased him, and will give you details of when your pup was last wormed. You should continue with regular worming – your vet will advise you on a sensible worming programme against roundworm, tapeworm, and, in some countries, heartworm.

Fleas

Your German Shepherd should also be treated regularly for fleas, particularly if he socialises with other dogs. There are many different products on the market that make it very easy to eradicate fleas – and keep them at bay, so there is no excuse for having a flea problem. Again, talk to your vet. Remember that your home should also be treated for fleas.

Health Care

Bloat

Bloat, where the stomach fills with gas, is a very serious condition that affects the larger breeds of dogs. Dogs that wolf their food down can be susceptible.

The dog will be uncomfortable and restless, and his sides will bulge. His breathing may also be affected. It can be fatal, so urgent veterinary attention should be sought if you suspect a problem.

Anal Furunculosis

This is a very nasty condition that can affect German Shepherds; it is rarely seen outside the breed. The region around the anus becomes very sore and infected, and, because of the way the tail is carried, the condition can remain undetected for some time. Check your German Shepherd's bottom regularly as part of his routine grooming care, and contact your vet if you notice anything unusual.

Joint Problems

The German Shepherd can be prone to a number of joint conditions, one of the most common being hip dysplasia, a painful condition of the hip joints. If you bought your dog from a reputable breeder, his parents will have had their hips evaluated. The methods vary in different countries, but your vet will explain the procedure to you.

If your German Shepherd has any sign that he is finding it difficult or painful to walk, you must consult a vet. There are a number of treatments that can be tried.

Remember that the German Shepherd is a large breed, and his joints are particularly vulnerable if you over-exercise him (see page 19).